S0-BSV-941

vjbnf   VAL
345.730773 MACHA

Machajewski, David, author
No cruel or unusual punishment
33410015456447   09/17/19

DISCARDED
Valparaiso - Porter County
Valparaiso Public Library
103 Jefferson Street
Library Valparaiso, IN 46383

OUR BILL OF RIGHTS

NO CRUEL OR UNUSUAL PUNISHMENT

A LOOK AT THE EIGHTH AMENDMENT

DAVID MACHAJEWSKI

PowerKiDS press

NEW YORK

Published in 2019 by The Rosen Publishing Group, Inc.
29 East 21st Street, New York, NY 10010

Copyright © 2019 by The Rosen Publishing Group, Inc.

All rights reserved. No part of this book may be reproduced in any form without permission in writing from the publisher, except by a reviewer.

Editor: Sharon Gleason
Book Design: Rachel Rising

Photo Credits: Cover Burlingham/Shutterstock.com; Cover, pp. 1, 3, 4, 6, 7, 8, 10, 11, 12, 13, 14, 15, 16, 17, 18, 20, 22, 23, 24, 25, 27, 28, 29, 30, 31, 32 (background) Mad Dog/Shutterstock.com; Cover, pp. 1, 3, 4, 6, 7, 8, 10, 11, 12, 13, 14, 15, 16, 17, 18, 20, 22, 23, 24, 25, 27, 28, 29, 30, 31, 32 (background) Flas100/Shutterstock.com; p. 5 Victor Moussa/Shutterstock.com; p. 6 Forest Foxy/Shutterstock.com; p. 7 iiiphevgeniy/Shutterstock.com; p. 9 f11photo/ Shutterstock.com; p. 11 Roman Babakin/Shutterstock.com; p. 13 Christopher Penler/Shutterstock.com; p. 14 boyphare/Shutterstock.com; p. 15 sirtravelalot/Shutterstock.com; p. 17 CaseyMartin/Shutterstock.com; p. 19 FOTOKITA/Shutterstock.com; p. 21 IR Stone/Shutterstock.com; p. 22 LightField Studios/Shutterstock.com; p. 23 txking/Shutterstock.com; p. 24 Andrea Izzotti/Shutterstock.com; p. 25 Print Collector/Hulton Fine Art Collection/ Getty Images; p. 27 Sebastian Duda/Shutterstock.com; p. 29 doomu/Shutterstock.com; p. 30 iMoved Studio/Shutterstock.com.

Cataloging-in-Publication Data

Names: Machajewski, David.
Title: No cruel or unusual punishment: a look at the eighth Amendment / David Machajewski.
Description: New York : PowerKids Press, 2019. | Series: Our Bill of Rights | Includes glossary and index.
Identifiers: ISBN 9781538343081 (pbk.) | ISBN 9781538343104 (library bound) | ISBN 9781538343098 (6 pack)
Subjects: LCSH: United States. Constitution. 8th Amendment--Juvenile literature. | Capital punishment--United States-- Juvenile literature. | Punishment--United States--Juvenile literature.
Classification: LCC KF4558 8th .M33 2019 | DDC 345.73'0772--dc23

Manufactured in the United States of America

CPSIA Compliance Information: Batch #CWPK19 For further information contact Rosen Publishing, New York, New York at 1-800-237-9932.

CONTENTS

WE THE PEOPLE

More than 200 years ago, a group of men who'd later be called the framers met in Philadelphia, Pennsylvania. Their goal was simple: they wanted to create rules that would guide the United States government. Although not all of the framers agreed with each other, they worked together to write the U.S. Constitution. After much **debate**, the states ratified, or approved, the Constitution.

The Constitution is one of the most important **documents** in American history. The Constitution created the three branches of the federal government: executive (the presidency), judicial (the courts), and legislative (Congress). The Constitution is like a map that tells us how the government works. The United States would be lost without it!

KNOW YOUR RIGHTS!

"To frame" means to shape or construct something. That's why the men who wrote the Constitution are sometimes called the framers.

THE FIGHT FOR OUR RIGHTS

The Constitution created a strong government, but some people were unhappy with it. Many believed that it was not specific enough about citizens' rights. A group of people called the anti-Federalists were worried that the Constitution would make the government too powerful and let the president rule like a king. People were worried about this issue because the United States had just gained independence from Great Britain, which was ruled by a monarchy.

The anti-Federalists believed that the Constitution needed to include rules about individual rights to ensure those rights were protected. Many stated they would only support the Constitution if promises about individual rights were included. In this way, the seeds of the Bill of Rights were being planted even before the Constitution became law.

Alexander Hamilton was an important member of the Federalists. You might recognize his face because his portrait is on the $10 bill.

FEDERALISTS VS. ANTI-FEDERALISTS

The anti-Federalists opposed the Federalists—a group of people who supported the Constitution as it was originally written. A few prominent members of the Federalists—Alexander Hamilton, James Madison, and John Jay—published a number of essays often called "the Federalist Papers" to try to convince certain states to ratify the Constitution.

JAMES MADISON PLAYS BOTH SIDES

After the Constitution was ratified, Founding Father and future president James Madison made an important proposal to the House of Representatives. He argued that there needed to be changes, or amendments, to the Constitution so that the rights of individuals would be protected.

Because of his support for individual rights, you might think Madison was an anti-Federalist. However, he was actually a proud Federalist at this point. Although he believed the Constitution didn't need to change, he knew amendments were needed to promote peace and prosperity in the new nation. He moved quickly to propose these amendments in order to satisfy the anti-Federalists so that they would stop criticizing and fighting against the Constitution.

KNOW YOUR RIGHTS!

James Madison was the fourth president of the United States, from 1809 until 1817.

James Madison made his case for the Bill of Rights inside Federal Hall in New York City. The building was demolished in 1812, and this new building opened on the site decades later.

POWER TO THE PEOPLE

Madison suggested several amendments (with many specific changes) to the Constitution. In time, the House approved 17 separate amendments. The Senate considered them but narrowed the number down to 12. The next step was to send these amendments to the individual states for approval. In the end, the states agreed to 10 amendments.

The first 10 amendments are combined into a single document called the Bill of Rights, which forms the foundation of the rights of the citizens of the United States.

Additional amendments to the Constitution have been added over time. Today, there are 27 amendments, and the latest amendment to the Constitution was added in 1992. It is very difficult to add an amendment to the Constitution, so they're rarely added. However, lawmakers propose new amendments frequently, so it's likely that the list of amendments will continue to grow.

Not all Americans were protected by the Bill of Rights. For example, the rights of slaves weren't addressed in this document. The Founding Fathers allowed slavery to continue because they believed that including laws supporting the rights of slaves would divide the country instead of uniting it. But, slavery was officially ended by the 13th Amendment at the end of the Civil War.

You can visit the Bill of Rights at the National Archives in Washington, D.C., which has many other national treasures on display.

BAIL, FINES, AND PUNISHMENT

Many Americans are familiar with certain amendments. For example, the First Amendment is famous because it protects the freedoms of religion, speech, press, and assembly. You have the right to believe, say, and do whatever you desire without punishment from the government because of this amendment—as long as you're not committing a crime.

However, some amendments aren't as well known because they protect people in more unusual situations. The Eighth Amendment is an example of an amendment that affects people in specific situations.

The Eighth Amendment says: "Excessive **bail** shall not be required, nor excessive fines imposed, nor cruel and unusual punishments **inflicted**." In the following chapters, we'll unpack this amendment further, exploring who it affects, what it means, and why it's sometimes **controversial**.

THE ORIGIN OF THE EIGHTH AMENDMENT

If you're confused about what the Eighth Amendment means, you're not alone. The amendment was borrowed almost word for word from the English Bill of Rights created in 1689, so the way it's written might sound outdated today.

The First Amendment protects many freedoms, including the freedom of speech.

UNDERSTANDING THE EIGHTH AMENDMENT

To understand the Eighth Amendment, it's important to know that it affects people who are accused or convicted of crimes. Criminal acts can be minor, such as when a person breaks a traffic law, but they can also be very serious, such as when someone purposely harms someone else.

Simple traffic **violations** aren't considered serious crimes. The punishment for a traffic violation is usually a fine, not jail time. In some states a traffic violation is considered an **infraction**, which is not a criminal act.

When someone commits a crime in the United States, they're usually punished by the criminal justice system. Not all crimes are treated equally, though. In general, the more harmful a crime is, the harsher the punishment. The Eighth Amendment sets rules that help make sure that punishments for crimes are fitting and reasonable.

How does the Eighth Amendment accomplish this? It's written with three **clauses**, each of which provides guidance on how to handle criminal actions.

EXCESSIVE BAIL SHALL NOT BE REQUIRED

The first part of the Eighth Amendment is called the excessive bail clause, and it sets rules about bail. When the police catch someone they believe committed a crime, that person may have to attend court in front of a judge or jury, who will decide if they're guilty or innocent. While they're waiting for their court date, defendants, or those officially accused of a crime, may be able to pay money so they don't have to sit in jail. This bail money's like a promise between the defendant and the court: their payment ensures they'll attend court and not try to escape, and they get their money back once they make their court dates.

The excessive bail clause in the Eighth Amendment helps make sure that bail isn't too expensive. Paying bail allows defendants to leave jail and prepare for their upcoming trial. It also relates to a central idea of the justice system: people shouldn't be punished until they're found innocent or guilty through a fair trial.

HOW DO JUDGES SET BAIL?

A judge decides the amount of bail by reviewing several factors. This usually includes how likely it is that a defendant will skip their court date, the type of crime a defendant is accused of committing, whether a defendant is considered dangerous, and the general safety of the community.

If you have played the board game Monopoly, you may have used a "get out of jail free" card. No such card exists in real life, and in order to leave jail, those charged with a crime must often pay bail.

Chance

THIS CARD MAY BE KEPT UNTIL NEEDED, OR SOLD

GET OUT OF JAIL FREE

©1936, 1996 Hasbro, Inc.

EXCESSIVE FOR SOME, AFFORDABLE FOR OTHERS

The excessive bail clause provides rules about how much bail costs, but it still affects people differently. Consider this: if a poor person is accused of a crime, even if the Eighth Amendment is followed, they might not be able to afford bail. Situations like this occur quite often and could upset people's lives. For example, suspects may lose their jobs or be unable to care for their family if they can't afford bail.

Studies have shown that if someone can't afford bail, they're more likely to plead guilty before their trial, even if they're innocent. Therefore, some people believe that bail can sometimes be used as a form of **discrimination** and that bail reform is needed to prevent discrimination. This type of inequality shows how the Eighth Amendment, and laws in general, can have different interpretations.

KNOW YOUR RIGHTS!

Studies show that the total number of people in jail falls when bail reform is put into effect.

If a person can't afford their bail, they're often left with no choice but to stay in jail until their court date, whether they're guilty or innocent.

NO EXCESSIVE FINES

The second part of the Eighth Amendment is similar to the excessive bail clause, but instead of dealing with bail, it addresses fines. When a suspect has been found guilty of a less serious crime, or misdemeanor, their punishment is often a fine, which is an amount of money owed to the government. The purpose of a fine is to punish the offender, but also to prevent that person from breaking the law again.

The excessive fine clause helps ensure that the amount of a fine fits the seriousness of the offense. In general, the more serious a crime is, the higher the fine will be. Judges usually require fines instead of jail time for minor crimes, but in some cases both punishments are required.

KNOW YOUR RIGHTS!

If you're thinking about pranking your friend by ordering pizza to their house without them knowing, think twice. In some states, you could be fined up to $500 for this type of prank!

If a driver goes through a red light and is caught, they usually won't be required to go to jail, but they'll usually need to pay a fine. This is because running a red light is usually considered an infraction.

CRUEL AND UNUSUAL PUNISHMENTS

The Eighth Amendment's final clause prevents the government from inflicting "cruel and unusual punishments" on people while they're in **custody**. This clause protects the rights of defendants and criminals when it comes to how they're treated by the police.

The "cruel and unusual punishment" clause is important for people who are in police custody.

While this might sound simple, this clause is highly controversial. This is because the framers kept this part of the amendment vague and open to interpretation: it's difficult for people to agree on when punishment is fitting and when it crosses the line into "cruel and unusual" territory.

Debates about this clause have existed since the Bill of Rights was ratified. We'll later see how these debates continue to affect people today, but first we'll look at this clause's history.

THE LEGACY OF "TITUS THE LIAR"

The words in the English Bill of Rights that inspired the Eighth Amendment may have been partly inspired by Titus Oates, an Englishman from the 1600s. Oates was nicknamed "Titus the Liar" because he made false claims about people. When Oates was sentenced for lying under oath, part of his punishment was public **humiliation**—not just one time, but once a year for the rest of his life.

TESTIS OVAT

Titus Oates was punished yearly by being locked in an old-fashioned device called a pillory in a public area. This was done to embarrass and humiliate him. Although they were common in the 1600s, pillories would be considered a cruel form of punishment today.

Some people considered this punishment unusually harsh because it was repeated annually. The case inspired English lawmakers to ban cruel and unusual punishment.

When it was America's turn to write a Bill of Rights in 1791, lawmakers decided to include similar language to make sure that the government wouldn't punish people in ways that didn't fit the crime. Although Oates's crime resulted in severe punishments, his case has an important **legacy**.

WHEN IS PUNISHMENT CRUEL AND UNUSUAL?

To help decide which punishments are fair for a certain crime, judges study history and rulings by the U.S. Supreme Court. The Supreme Court is the highest court in the United States. When these judges, known as justices, oversee a criminal case, they interpret the laws and amendments of the Constitution and make decisions about what the law means.

These decisions influence how other judges interpret laws. For example, in 1972, a Supreme Court justice said, in his opinion, that if a punishment was too severe for a crime, or if it was socially unacceptable, then it crossed the line into cruel and unusual territory.

By looking at previous court cases, justices today know that punishments should correspond to the type of crime that was committed. If a person robbed a bank and hurt people in the process, they would likely face a long jail sentence. But a judge today would not sentence a person to life in prison for a parking ticket. That's because judges have learned from history that harmless crimes don't deserve such serious penalties.

GETTING TO KNOW THE SUPREME COURT

The Constitution is sometimes difficult to understand, so Supreme Court justices are constantly studying it. Also, since many laws and amendments were written long ago, justices help apply these old laws to modern times. What may have been legal 200 years ago might not make sense in today's world, so Supreme Court justices help make sure the law protects the rights of people today.

Supreme Court justices **uphold** and interpret the Constitution, which includes the Bill of Rights.

THE DEBATE OVER CAPITAL PUNISHMENT

Capital punishment is one of the most highly debated punishments today. In the United States, it is reserved for those who are convicted of capital crimes such as murder.

Some people who approve of the death penalty believe it gives **closure** to victims' families, and that it prevents similar crimes from happening again. On the other hand, those who disapprove of it argue that sentencing someone to death is extremely cruel and violates the cruel and unusual punishment clause.

Now that we've explored the Eighth Amendment, do you think capital punishment violates it? Or do you believe that the death penalty is a fair punishment for a person convicted of a capital crime? There are no right or wrong answers to these questions, but when we debate these points of view, it helps us get closer to offering fitting punishments for all types of crimes.

A debate helps people on different sides of an issue understand each other's point of view.

KNOW YOUR RIGHTS!

Even though the death penalty is allowed by the Constitution, several states have banned capital punishment because of their interpretation of the Eighth Amendment. As of 2018, 19 states and Washington, D.C., have banned the death penalty.

THE EIGHTH AMENDMENT TODAY

The Eighth Amendment plays a vital role in making sure that citizens' rights are protected. Its inclusion in the Bill of Rights shows how important the Founding Fathers treated the issue of how our government punishes criminal actions. By exploring the Eighth Amendment's three clauses, we see how it guides judges and law enforcement.

To this day, the Eighth Amendment ensures that bail, fines, and punishment are fair and not too severe. And if a person believes they've been punished too harshly while in custody, they can use the Eighth Amendment to support their claims in court. Interpretations of the Eighth Amendment don't always have a right answer but studying and debating its contents remains an important part of ensuring justice for all U.S. citizens.

GLOSSARY

bail: Money or property provided to make sure that a suspect released from custody will return to court at a later time.

capital punishment: The legal killing of a convicted person as punishment for a crime; also referred to as the death penalty.

clause: A specific section of a document that makes a statement. The Eighth Amendment has three clauses.

closure: A feeling that a bad experience has ended and that you can start to live again in a calm and normal way.

controversial: Likely to give rise to disagreement.

custody: Another word for imprisonment. Criminal suspects are "taken into custody" by police when they're accused of committing a crime.

debate: A discussion in which people express different opinions, or to discuss different opinions about something.

discrimination: Different, unfair treatment based on factors such as a person's race, age, religion, or gender.

document: A formal piece of writing.

humiliation: To make someone feel ashamed and foolish, especially publicly.

inflict: To cause someone to experience or be affected by something unpleasant or harmful.

infraction: The breaking of a minor rule or law.

legacy: Something that comes from someone in the past.

uphold: To confirm or support something.

violation: A case of failing to respect someone's rights.

INDEX

WEBSITES

Due to the changing nature of Internet links, PowerKids Press has developed an online list of websites related to the subject of this book. This site is updated regularly. Please use this link to access the list: www.powerkidslinks.com/obor/eighth